Set This Butterfly Free

Transforming Your Relationship with Energy, Money, and Life!

Jan Litterst

Copyright © 2021 Jan Litterst

All rights reserved. No part of this publication may be reproduced, distributed, or transmitted in any form or by any means, including photocopying, recording, or other electronic or mechanical methods, without the prior written permission of the copyright owner, except provided by the United States of America copyright law.

Published by Your Shift Matters Publishing.

Printed in the United States of America.
Print ISBN: 978-1-7378234-0-7

This publication is designed to provide accurate and authoritative information regarding the subject matter covered. It is sold with the understanding that the publisher is not engaged in rendering legal, accounting, or other professional advice. If legal advice or other expert assistance is required, the services of a competent professional should be sought. The opinions expressed by the authors in the book are not endorsed by Your Shift Matters Publishing and are the sole responsibility of the author rendering the opinion.

Formatting and cover design by www.letsgetbooked.com

CONTENTS

Foreword 5
Introduction 7
A Guide to Get Started 11
Your Basic Energy Money Tool....................................... 14
The Green Circle of Energy 17
The Apple Green Circle of Work 19
Excellence, Empowerment and Magnified Energy 21
The Hierarchy of Needs Pyramid 23
The Real Difference Between Your Needs & Wants 26
When Needs and Wants Change 31
Wants and Needs or Needs and Wants? 36
Money Needs Energy 47
Does Your Energy Want You to Be Rich?....................... 58
Be Ready for Conflict: The Red Boxing Gloves 62
Money: A Symbol of Life Force Energy 68
Money Energy: Shifting Your Energy Through Faith 75
Breathing in Love and Faith 79
Letting Go!.. 85
Busy, Busy, Busy… Stop it!.. 91
Butterflies Are Meant to Be Free 94
Emptying Our Mind 97
Energy and Moving Forward 100
Energy and Gratitude 103
About the Author 106

Foreword

I first met Jan Litterst 20 years ago at the Unity Spiritual Center in Westlake, Ohio, where I am an ordained Unity Minister. Over the years, I watched as she reinvented herself many times, always with the courage to follow her heart. Even as she was pointed in different directions, she always pursued her goal to help others. As I got to know her better, we talked about her seminars, classes, and the work she did in the community, including giving prosperity classes at church.

When I received a small inheritance, I went to Jan for advice because of her strong financial background. She gave me the confidence to begin investing and the journey to financial freedom began. For the last five years, I have enjoyed my retirement in Florida partly because of Jan and her guidance through the process of creating financial independence.

I particularly like her goal to raise women's consciousness and to help them prepare for the future. To reach this goal, Jan has a developed a set of steps to achieve financial freedom. Her concept has five stages: energy, work, excellence, empower, and magnified energy.

These steps educate and encourage the reader to take the journey to financial security. It is a growth process that works for everyone beginning with that first concept that money is simply energy. In this book, Jan gives many examples and anecdotes to illustrate her points clearly and to help you apply these concepts in your own life. The exercises prompt you to understand your thoughts and feelings regarding money and how it affects your needs and wants. The method works if you do the work.

Her choice of the butterfly is a powerful symbol for freeing your Spirit. This book not only speaks to freeing your Spirit around money but applies to every part of life; relationships, health, business, spiritual growth, creativity, and any part of life you would like to unleash and set free.

This book will guide you through the stages of achieving your own wealth and beginning the journey to financial freedom.

Barbara Smith
Ordained Minister
Unity Spiritual Center
Westlake, Ohio

Introduction

Financial wellness is not about savings, checking, or investment accounts. It's about feeling at peace with your money, no matter how much money you have. It's about understanding that you can have power with your money rather than pad a financial company's bottom line.

The fall of 2010 was a powerful time for me. It led to many changes in my life, including a departure from the traditional world of financial services. From 1994, I had been in bank management and worked as a financial planner in several of the large wirehouses of Wall Street and Main Street. My passion was to help people with their money, and I did. For anyone who has experience with financial services, helping clients is what the advertising campaigns talk about. However, the main goal for the banks and investment companies is to make a profit. This was not what mattered most to me.

I left that role to focus on helping women gain understanding, confidence, and empowerment with their money. It is my goal to help them create financial wellness. That same year I was challenged to create a basic financial literacy program for homeless women in Cleveland. It was through this challenge that the *Empower Excellence* program came to be. With divine guidance, I created a program about *needs and wants*, which is a concept developed years ago in Abraham Maslow's Hierarchy of Needs.

The concept of clearly defined needs and wants is the true foundation of financial literacy, more fundamental than saving, investing, and budgeting. It is creating and understanding how you can focus your mind and simplify decisions about money. It is the foundation of financial wellness for your lifetime. No matter how simple or complex a money decision you are facing, it is the starting point that you can return to as often as you need it.

This book is not a basic financial literacy how-to, although I will touch on those topics.

This book is your guide to understanding that money is energy. *The Energy of Money*, birthed by Maria Nemeth, PhD. in the 1990's, was a source of enlightenment for me. I have recommended her work to thousands over the years as I put the energy of money to work in my personal life and the lives of my clients. Her work is deep and comprehensive. It is time for a more uplifting view of how peace and power can come as a result of an individual's work with the energy of money. *Set This Butterfly Free* intends to walk you through your journey of transforming your personal relationship with money. It provides the basic framework for decision-making with money and the tools to understand and embrace your own money energy.

Money is in your life! It is in every aspect of your life. It can be your friend, an energy that makes life easier, better, and more enjoyable. However, it can also be your enemy emitting negative energy that adds stress, worry, heartbreak, and physical illness. As you read this book, you will learn how to change that energy and bring peace and power into your feelings about money. You can empower and transform your relationship with money, allowing yourself to feel good about money no matter how much money – or how little - you have.

Know that money has no energy of its own. We provide the energy money *appears to have*. Money is inanimate and was created as barter. We give it energy through our emotions and the meaning that we assign to it.

This is a journey. It's a journey I have traveled alone over the years, as the single parent of two sons. It's not a journey that I wish to have you travel alone. Know that I am here with you on this journey, and it is a journey traveling towards peace and power and love in your relationship with money.

Jan Litterst

A Guide to Get Started

As you prepare to *Set This Butterfly Free*, there are a few things that will help you on your journey. I recommend you choose some writing materials: simple notebook paper, lined tablets, or a special binder. It's ideal if you have two journals so you can flow through this process- a Money Journal and a Gratitude Journal. Throughout this book, there will be transformational exercises in both categories - money and gratitude. When doing the exercises, use your favorite writing instruments: anything from colored pens and pencils to markers to crayons. You will find your style as you move on!

Let's get started.

The logo you see on the back cover is the logo of *Empower Excellence*, which represents my business. We will refer to it throughout this book. It evolved from a real experience in my life that occurred at the same time as my involvement in Brian Swimme's "The Powers of the Universe" program, presented locally by Maureen Gaughan Haggerty at River's Edge in Cleveland and Unity Spiritual Center in Westlake, Ohio.

Let's start at the top with the green circle. This circle represents energy. Without energy, nothing happens. It's similar to waking up in the morning, and the first thing you need to do is exert energy to wake up fully before you can do anything else.

The next circle, apple green, is the work you need to do to move ahead. In the example of your morning awakening, this is the work you must do to arise from your bed. Even though it may be a little piece of work, you will improve every time you repeat it.

At the five o'clock position of the logo is the turquoise circle which represents the excellence you create because of the work and the energy you have given to this one action.

The blue circle, which appears next, represents your feeling of empowerment once you have achieved excellence with this one action. That empowerment leads to the creation of more energy, represented by the purple circle. This is the energy that accumulates and brings you back to your original point of energy, which can now be put into action to focus on your next selected area of work.

The butterfly, in the center of the logo, represents the transformation that occurs as you repeat the energy-work-excellence-empower-energy cycles! When you are familiar with the energy areas, turn your attention to the butterfly in the center. The butterfly is a symbol of transformation, and energy feeds that transformation. It is not an immediate and one-time infusion of energy. It is a transformation that occurs one step at a time. While the butterfly will remain in the center of the logo, the butterfly symbolically will be set free in your process of creating your own energy. Why? Because you will create the environment for the caterpillar to become the butterfly that you can become! Start your process to *Set This Butterfly Free*.

You can repeat the cycle infinitely, and the transformation you will experience will be ever-changing. It is powerful when you focus on this cycle and take the time to think through the process. It can put you in total control of everything you want to accomplish in your life.

This is the cycle of *Empower Excellence*. It is my work, and it demonstrates the flow of energy. This flow of energy moves a caterpillar through the work of becoming a butterfly; it is this flow of energy that can transform your life.

Your Basic Energy Money Tool

Life evolves! From the first moment of the Universe 14 billion years ago, or the first moment of your life, life evolves.

What powers all evolution is energy. Energy is what powers evolution, and energy powers life. It is sacred within each of us. It is that divine spark that we share with the Universe that connects us to each other. There are both simple and more complex manifestations of energy. An example would be taking a metaphysical concept or abstract thought or subject such as existence, causality, or truth and allow it to be powered by energy to become a physical reality.

Mastering energy, on the personal level or the universal level, is a matter of focus. Focusing consciously is the basis of many metaphysical activities, including the power of attraction.

It is a concept that each of us, by virtue of the Divine spark within us, can create our own reality. We share the same divine spark, for we were all present, and we were all one when the Universe came into existence. We all share energy. It was powerful at the moment of The Big Bang, and it is just as powerful today within each one of us.

Brian Swimme's work, "The Powers of the Universe," became a powerful part of my life in 2010. This electrifying work changed my life forever. It reflects the Universe story, the Big Bang, or Creation, depending upon your belief system. To demonstrate, here are simple illustrations of "The Powers".

Centration	Birth to a New Being
Allurement	Gravitational Attraction
Emergence	Creativity
Transmutation	Always Transcending
Transformation	Entire Community Changing
Interrelatedness	Care & Nurturing
Radiance	The Magnificence of the Universe

Each of "The Powers" flows into the next and the cycle keeps repeating in the Universe story and in each one of us. It is the way that everything continues to evolve.

Starting Your Journey

Take money energy slowly! Step by step. Start small. Grow with each thought and step you take. This is the cycle of *Empower Excellence*. This is my process in life and demonstrates the flow of energy. This flow of energy is what allows for the simple, yet complex, evolution of caterpillar to the butterfly. This type of energy can transform your life. The butterfly symbolizes transformation. That is why I chose it to be the center of the logo, and it is also why you will see this same butterfly at the end of each chapter moving you forward to the next step.

The following short chapters titled for each of the circles in the cycle–energy, work, excellence, empower, and energy magnified– explain their purpose in your own energy transformation.

Take each section slow, learn it, and begin to see how breaking down change into small pieces makes sense.

Later, you will see a variety of transformational opportunities. Commit yourself to work through those sections. One of the beauties of this process is that you can come back later, do the work repeatedly and see how you are changing and transforming. This book is perpetual because you are the one changing!

Breathe…Reflect…Transform…

The Green Circle of Energy

Let's start at the top of the cycle with the light green circle, which is *energy*. There is a tendency for anyone who begins energy work, especially about money, to want to do everything at once. Please do not be tempted. While it took years for you to become who you are with energy and money, it will not take a whole life to change it. However, it will work better if you take this one step at a time, determine if it is working or not, and then begin to transform it into what you would like it to be.

My grandson, Liam, is 6 years old. He knew nothing about money, but he could recognize his name when the mailman brought mail before he was two. He loved watching the mail fall through the slot to the porch. Beyond recognizing his name, there was little more the mail meant to him.

The opportunity was there for him to create energy with money. Working with my son, his father, we made a bank for him out of a shoe box! Liam was told to check the mail the next time it came and, when he did, he found an envelope with a one-dollar bill in it, which he put in his 'bank'.

Liam took one trip around the circle of money energy. Still no clue what this was all about, Liam now had more reason to look for the mail with his name on it so he could find the money and put it into his 'bank'. One step at a time, it was that simple. He learned that when he had his second birthday, the money was now two one-dollar bills. By then, he was learning to play games on his mother's iPad. But he quickly told me that all the games had to have the word "f-r-e-e" on them. And then, as his bank grew, he began to see that he could spend his money on iPad games for children. One step at a time.

Fast forward, now there are two grandsons. Liam, as the big brother, begins to teach his brother Kurty about money. He is now four, and both receive one-dollar bills when they open the mail from their GramGram Jan.

The momentum continues each trip around the circle as he takes his energy, works a little with it, becomes excellent with the knowledge he acquires. Liam is empowered!

Now he:

1. Collects piggy banks of all sorts.
2. Manipulates his brother to give him banks.
3. Asks visitors for change.
4. Wants "coins to fill his banks" for Christmas.
5. Teaches his brother all he has learned.
6. Saves his money, rather than spend it!

Liam learned about energy without ever having seen the word or knowing what it is. He just learned one step at a time, and now he is empowered with money energy.

The Apple Green Circle of Work

Continuing to move in small steps, the *work circle* in the cycle moves you forward. I invite you to think about this in simple terms.

When we awaken in the morning, we do not automatically eject ourselves from our comfy bed- if it could be that simple! Hitting "snooze" may be a small piece of work you need to do to allow you to roll over and put off the inevitable result of getting out of bed, but eventually, the next small piece of work requires putting our feet on the floor to move forward with our day. That is *work*!

Over the years, doing it day by day, most of us have become excellent at getting out of bed. How does this translate to you and your transformation with money?

1. Identify one small piece of work with money energy that you would like to transform, no matter how small it is.
2. Identify simple steps that can be done to achieve the desired transformation.

It may be deciding that your morning coffee, usually from a local coffee shop, could be replaced with a cup from home. While coffee is not free, it is much more economical to buy a bag of coffee at the grocery store. You can buy it already ground, or grind it yourself, and for less than $10 and have coffee for many days. You even have the smell of coffee to greet you at home! Consciously doing the work of buying your choice of coffee, grinding the beans at the grocery store, and brewing it at home, is the *work*.

It may save you a considerable amount over a year. For example, let's say you were buying a cup of coffee on your way to work each morning for $2. If you work 20 days a month, that's $40 a month and $480 a year. If you buy one bag of coffee a month for $10, you could save $360.

However, the more important part of the work is creating more energy through these small efforts of *work*.. You are feeling energetic enough to move on.

Breathe…Reflect…Transform

Excellence, Empowerment and Magnified Energy

Wow, you have discovered how little energy it takes to start making a change in your life. That energy moves you to do a small piece of work that, with each repetition, awakens your sense of *excellence,* represented by the turquoise circle in the cycle. With some conscious discipline, you will keep getting better and better. Remember, you are only doing one piece of work at a time, using only a tiny amount of energy with each repetition. The resulting *excellence*—and you will become excellent when you do not give up—*empowers you,* represented by the blue circle, and that, my friend, results in *magnified energy,* the purple circle.

Now it's quite possible that your mind is identifying other parts of your life that could benefit from Money Energy. This is a good thing! But remember to take one small step at a time. You identified how energy could be used to change one feeling or behavior. You did it, and you found that you became excellent at it. Pretty simple so far, right? How does it feel?

Stop and think about how you feel about accomplishing what you decided to transform, and now you make a great cup of coffee. Not only did you learn what you could do, you made a decision, stuck to it, and are saving money doing it. So, think of all the other changes you might want to make, no matter how small, taking it one step at a time.

It's essential to stop and acknowledge your feelings. Feelings are what can make a difference in your self-esteem, and it starts small! Ask yourself regularly throughout the day, "How do I feel?"

As women, we often don't stop and think about how we feel. By asking yourself, "How do I feel?" your head, your heart, and your soul must stop and think about it for a change. Doing so puts you on a new path of acknowledging what is going on with you, both bad and good.

Feelings of *empowerment* are powerful! As Baker Mayfield said after one of his first victorious games with the Cleveland Browns in 2018, "I feel dangerous!" And that is good. It indicates the power that you are developing internally. But more than that, *empowerment* leads to creating more energy, or *magnified energy*, in the deep purple circle of the cycle. Purple is a power color, a color of royalty. When the energy accumulates and brings you back to your original point of energy, it's a *royal feeling*. You can put this energy into action and shift your focus on the next area of work you'd like to tackle.

The Hierarchy of Needs Pyramid

Abraham Harold Maslow is the creator the Hierarchy of Needs which is a 5-tier pyramid model of human *needs* and *wants*. The lower levels of the pyramid, our basic *needs*, must be satisfied first before an individual can focus on things that are higher up, which are our *wants*.

The foundation of finding peace and power in your relationship with money is to recognize the work he did in identifying the cornerstones of our relationship with money as it pertains to our needs.

I have simplified Maslow's Hierarchy of Needs for the purposes of this book. However, you can find his original work in thousands of college textbooks and research papers. That is not what we are focusing on here. We are focusing on needs and wants, which did originate with Abraham's work and left a forever indelible mark on me as I pursued my major in organizational development many years ago. Needs and wants are very, very basic. It is where all thought about human development rests.

The foundation of the pyramid, level one, lies along the baseline with physical needs and safety. If the foundation does not exist as a strong starting point, the rest could topple. So, needs are first, and wants follow.

We refer to physical needs as basic food, clothing, and shelter. You might include air, water, sleep, and sex as well. Safety needs, level two, include shelter from harm, and can be found in societal order, in a stable family unit, and the laws of any community.

Love, the third level, represents family from birth, whether it is a natural or an adoptive family, and it also includes affection, caring, and devotion. Later in life, it can include teams or work groups. It is about the basic acceptance and care by others.

The fourth level, self-esteem, represents self-respect as well as the respect of others. It is how the world sees you in your eyes. It is how you see beauty, balance, and form in your life. You can realize transcendence with self-fulfilled personal growth and beliefs that lead you upward through the tiers of the pyramid to the higher levels. It can also include guiding others with you on this journey as well. The fifth level, self-actualization, is mainly expansion and mastery.

It is important to realize where you are on this pathway upwards. Wherever you are, accept that. It doesn't mean that you can't move forward. It just means that you need to understand and accept where you are currently. It is the only way you can effectively meet your current needs. The act of self-acceptance helps build your self-esteem over time.

Keep in mind that your needs are one thing, but your wants are always there too. In Maslow's own words, "Man is a perpetually wanting animal!" Needs and wants are the basics in your relationship with money. Keep them near and dear to your heart but recognize the difference as we proceed on this journey. Needs are your basic requirements for life. While some people may have a different view of *basic,* we can all agree that food, water, and shelter are needs. Wants are desirable pieces of your life, and they fall into place after the needs are met. Wants are desires, whether monetary, physical, or emotional and this can vary greatly. Needs are necessary for most people to function well in their lives. Functioning is very different than wanting!

The Real Difference Between Your Needs & Wants

"Money is only a tool. It will take you wherever you wish, but it will not replace you as the driver."

Ayn Rand

When I walked away from the financial services industry almost a decade ago, I fulfilled both a need and a want. I needed to be true to my passion and my soul. I also wanted to help people become financially well.

I wanted to help people with their money but in a very different way. When people stress about money, they may not always know the reason why. They are just stressed. They may always stress about money. Perhaps they don't want to make money decisions, so they pass off their money decisions to their financial professionals. Or maybe they feel they made money decisions by allowing their financial professionals to make their decisions for them.

Yes, clients need to have good financial professionals; but clients need to understand their choices and decisions. Fear, avoidance, escape, and hate, among other emotions, often stop them from participating in their financial decisions. Rather than address the emotions, people acquiesce. They choose to ignore them and avoid making a decision. However, the unresolved feelings remain and continue to surface whenever a decision needs to be made.

While well-known 'money experts' such as David Bach and Suze Orman provide a great deal of financial education, they ignore the underlying emotions. Consequently, the cycle of ignoring the underlying emotions keeps repeating itself. This is why people turn to these personalities in an attempt to find the solution to their money problems. They don't understand why they can't overcome them.

I saw many clients who would tell me, "Jan, make the decision for me. Just let me know what you decide." It was a rude awakening to them to hear me say that I would not decide for them. What I offered instead, was a discussion to uncover why they would not, or could not, make decisions about their money themselves. At first, they would dance around any discussion until the fear diminished, and they felt they could trust me. Finally, in their own time, they could make decisions for themselves!

Many of my clients were divorced women. Bettina had been divorced for three years when I met her. She had read an article that mentioned me in a local magazine and felt she could relate to me, so we arranged a time to meet. Surprisingly, she arrived with three of her brothers who were helping her with her financial decisions. Before her marriage, her father was the one that helped her. During her marriage, her spouse made all the financial decisions.

Bettina wanted to learn how to manger her finances by herself, but it was easier to let the men in her life do it for her. Hesitant and scared, she wanted to work with me, but the brothers were uncertain that she should change anything. End of story? No.

Two years later, we met again, but this time she came in by herself. Step by step, I worked with her to understand every decision she had to make. Step by step, she began to understand her finances better. Bettina became a butterfly set free!

She was plagued by the fear of not knowing what to do because no one ever allowed her to make her own financial decisions. Clients like Bettina convinced me that there was a major need to create an environment of financial wellness for them.

Clients like Bettina created the energy that generates Empowered Excellence. There was a need to help people uncover their money stories. There was a need to work with people to develop an understanding of how to make money decisions. Additionally, there was a need to create financial wellness as a way to have a peaceful and powerful relationship with money.

Currently, to make the programs personal and private, most *Empower Excellence* programs are available online and through individual coaching programs. I also offer the programs in corporate settings and community groups. The two main programs of *Empower Excellence* are:

- Energize Your Life, Energize Your Money
- The Empower Program

Making confident money decisions is seeing the transformation from a caterpillar to a confident beautiful butterfly. But *setting the butterfly free* is not always easy when it comes to money and financial decisions!

There are many reasons men and women fail to take the time to discover and solve their fears about money. From a young age, both men and women are exposed to family, cultural, religious, educational, and mythical beliefs about money, often unexplained to them. They then grow up with those beliefs holding them back from making confident decisions as adults. They simply weren't taught how to make decisions about money, much less other life decisions. So, when faced with transitions in life, careers, relationships, and more, they are missing the tools that would give them the needed confidence and self-esteem to feel good about their decisions.

Those childhood fears can impact us into adult life. Making time in our busy lives to tackle emotional issues may be uncomfortable, to say the least. Most people will find every excuse not to make time to do this.

Money is involved in every part of our lives. Not making a decision is a decision in itself. That means someone else, or an event, decides for you and you've given away your energy.

Money is everywhere and inherent in everything you do in life, so you must be involved. Of course, the degree of involvement in any part of your life can vary; but money is a constant in our lives.

Basic needs require money, and people acquire it in various ways—through a paycheck, an inheritance, public assistance, and illegal means, for example. No matter where the money comes from, there are decisions to be made. It can seem daunting to determine what your needs are. As humans, we often focus on our wants first. It's up to you to make those decisions.

The *Energize* and *Empower* programs work to energize, empower, and help people with their money. The programs provide fundamental financial literacy tools and an emotional tool kit that helps to build your confidence with money. These tools can put you on a journey to prosperity and abundance, which includes so much more than just money. It's also the pathway to a life of love rather than a life of fear.

It is all about you and money. Maslow provides the backdrop to guide you to a life where it all finally makes sense.

Breathe…Reflect…Transform.

When Needs and Wants Change

"I was wise enough to never grow up, while fooling people into believing I had."

Margaret Mead

Jenita is a young lady who attended one of my EMPOWER programs. Young and single, she worked at a minimum wage job and was working to complete her GED program to improve her life. She struggled to meet her physical needs with her small paycheck. However, it was apparent that Jenita was proud of her physical appearance, especially her freshly and regularly manicured nails.

In the class discussion about needs and wants, there were differing opinions on whether a manicure was a need or a want. Obviously, not all agreed. Jenita, however, stood her ground and defended her position that her weekly manicure was a need.

Curious about her rationale, I encouraged her to explain. For Jenita, manicured nails made her feel good about herself. It was her way to stay mentally healthy, to maintain her self-esteem. It was a form of love that she gave to herself and far less expensive than mental health counseling. I had to agree. For Jenita, a manicure was a need.

Checking back with the Pyramid earlier in the book, we did not talk about actualization and transcendence. These are processes that can occur throughout needs and wants. When it comes to actualization and transcendence, you can be working in these areas with or without money.

Simply defined, transcendence is going beyond the limits of your mindset, physically or emotionally, surpassing an object, and becoming independent of the world. Transcendence is a more metaphysical and supernatural term than many mentioned here. For me, it is a 'spiritual' term. It's not wise to think that the higher you are in the pyramids, the more money you will have. However, it's interesting to encounter someone who may be focusing on actualization and transcendence when they have not mastered physical needs, safety, love, and self-esteem.

Mick was an example of this conundrum. Oh, he was charming and appeared to be the epitome of actualization and transcendence. He came into my life in the best of all possible ways, through an activity related to my church. We began a friendship that grew into a simple relationship.

He was proud of the fact that he was a self-made millionaire three times over. However, he sensed my disbelief and provided documentary proof. Interesting! More interesting was that he lost all the money three times over.

Mick lived out of state, and he soon had to leave to go back home. What I learned was that he had no home to go back to. As entrepreneurial as he was, he had no doubt that everything would be okay. That said, it was apparent to everyone who cared about Mick that there was no money to back up that belief. He needed money to meet his basic needs.

We had built a strong relationship based on our shared spiritual beliefs. We talked daily until the calls stopped when he was put in jail as a vagrant in his own upscale community. He eventually moved in with a friend to try to rebuild his life. He needed money.

We began talking again, although not because he needed money. He became a teacher of metaphysical and spiritual matters for me. He was impressive, enlightening, and appeared to be self-actualized and totally in a state of transcendence.

The relationship grew, fueled in part by trips by both of us to and from his state. However, during those visits, it became apparent that he genuinely lacked basic physical needs, safety, love, and self-esteem. I learned that his condo was not his condo, his refrigerator was empty, and he was being evicted. He lost all of his personal possessions and had nowhere to go. Even his leased car getting repossessed. His physical needs were not being met. Mick needed money but refused to do anything about it. More than that, Mick had already been divorced and was estranged from his sons and their families. So, love was absent as well.

Still to this day, he exemplified transcendence while never establishing a stable foundation. He was at a higher intellectual level, but his feet never touched the ground. There are people who work with others on a spiritual level while unable to meet their own basic needs. It may be an escape from reality but, no matter what, money is needed.

It takes money to take care of your physical needs. When you achieve that foundation, you are free to develop yourself as you move upwards through the tiers. You can minimize your need for money in many ways as you do this (remember the coffee example). One important way is to realize that your abundance or prosperity consists of so much more than money.

Many people feel that money will come to them as they move toward actualization and transcendence. Safety, love, and self-esteem are important and necessary to reach the highest tiers, but they can't be bought with money. It's important to pay attention to this when teaching children about money.

Children need to feel love and belonging. They can receive this from family, whatever the definition of 'family' might be. Not all children receive love and belonging from their families. It can also come from friends and relationships outside of the family. They receive their physical needs from the adults in their lives when they are children. If the physical needs aren't met, the foundation for the child will be shaky going forward. Some money problems may arise as children try to compensate for not receiving love or the feeling of belonging in their families.

An essential part of childhood is to grow and mature into adults and understand that their physical needs must be met. When they become adults, they need to make sure these needs are met first.

According to their personal values, each person must decide whether something is a need, or a want. Then they have to decide how they're going to pay for them. This is rarely taught to children when they begin to make some decisions of their own, which is at the preschool age. Consequently, as adults, they are still at a loss about money because they never learned basic decision-making skills as a child. They don't know how to differentiate between needs and wants or how to pay for them.

Breathe…Reflect…Transform.

Wants and Needs or Needs and Wants?

'Needs and wants', as a phrase, doesn't roll off the tongue as easily as 'wants and needs'. For years, I can remember the phrase 'wants and needs' being used all the time. It could be that, subconsciously, this is how we prefer to prioritize the two, putting wants before needs. We know that needs have to come first, for they sustain our life.

A baby's needs, starting at birth, are quite simple. One of their first needs is water. In fact, a human baby is three-quarters water! Barbara Kingsolver states this as a matter of fact:

"Water is life. It is the briny broth of our origins, the pounding circulatory system of the world. We stake our civilizations on the coasts and mighty rivers. Our deepest dread is the threat of having too little—or too much." Yet, water is a basic human need.

Food is also a need. The human body needs nourishment through food in addition to water. The quality of life is highly dependent upon the quality of food available. Volumes have been written on this topic alone: local food, industrial food, vegan, vegetarian, carnivore, and the millions of different diets available. It is undeniable that water and food are basic needs of our daily life. It is also undeniable that the money available to an individual determines the quality and quantity available to each of us.

In addition to water and food, what other needs do we have to exist? Shelter is also a need. The size of our shelter and whether we own or rent, correlates to the money we have available. The final basic need is clothing. Just as with water and food, the money available to us determines what kind of clothing we can choose.

When Needs and Wants Blur

That Begins with Childhood!

It would appear that paying for food, shelter, and clothing would be an easy financial decision. But there is another factor that affects money decisions—emotions and feelings!

Let's not overlook the influence of emotions surrounding decisions about money in all stages of life. An adult's emotions complicate decisions for even very young children, affecting them for the rest of their lives. Keep in mind that it is not the baby's emotions but the emotions of the adults who are making decisions for the baby. The adults are parents, family, and doctors. Ideally, they all have an emotional tie to the baby, and an emotional value is placed on the baby's life just as it is on the lives of all of those we love. There are circumstances where medical care are needs for a baby. Over time, what used to be wants have become needs because of the advances in the medical profession. There are times when extraordinary means are taken to extend a baby's life when they don't have a chance to survive otherwise. Is this a need or a want? There again, it becomes a question of the values of the person making the decision.

Needs and Wants from Childhood to Adulthood

The emotional side of decision making for needs and wants continues as the child grows. Most parents want to provide not only the needs of their child but also to provide everything they want for the child. Eventually, they provide everything the child, itself, wants. In many cases, it is the parent's need or want, not the child's. It is the parent's desire to give their child everything, whether it's a need or a want, and whether or not they have the money to provide it.

Sooner or later, the parents will hopefully begin to teach their child the difference between needs and wants; however, parents cannot teach what they have not learned. It becomes systemic when this occurs over generations. If they are ineffective in teaching their children about needs and wants, the cycle continues.

Many parents love lavishing their children with material goods. Sometimes, it's to show that they love their child. But it also stems from how they experienced love growing up. Either way, it complicates the child's ability to learn the difference between needs and wants.

Parents who want to do the right thing for their children may have difficulty discerning between needs and wants. They try to do the right thing, but they are not consistent in setting the example and providing teachable moments for their child. As a result, the child grows up unable to make decisions between needs and wants, thus the cycle continues!

My goal is to prepare preschool children and their parents to make decisions about needs and wants on the individual and family levels. The child is a part of the family, and each family member, while being aware of their own individual needs, must also be mindful of the family's needs as a unit. It is not uncommon to see a child in a department store vigorously expressing a want or a need. Unfortunately, the child often cannot differentiate between the two and shows frustration by having temper tantrums.

Envision the following short exchange between a parent and a child:

Child: "I want this!"

Parent: "No, we cannot buy that today."

Child: "But I want it!"

Parent: "I told you, we cannot buy that today."

Child: "I need this. I need this!"

Parent: "I do not have the money for that."

Child: "But I need it, and I'm going to buy it!" (Putting the object in the cart)

Parent: "No!" (Taking the item out of the cart)

And then the tantrum is in full motion. The outcome can go in many different ways. The frustration level of both child and parent is highly emotional, with the child feeling deprived and the parent feeling less than sufficient at parenting. Strangers often add their disapproving looks and comments, adding negative energy to the whole scene.

Children need to know that their needs and wants are important, but they also need to learn that the parent is in control, and it is the parent's responsibility to make the decisions for the family unit. It is often hard to explain the concept of needs and wants to a young child. But it is essential that both the child and the parents learn the concept of needs and wants to master the topic of money together.

If this activity does not occur at a young age, the battle between the needs and wants of the child and the parent will continue into the teenage years, the young adult years, and even into the mature adult years. The child becomes entitled to whatever the child needs or wants regardless of what their parents think. Throughout the lives of parents and the child, the parent may always be the parent emotionally. They may always want to take care of their child. However, it is the parents' role to prepare the child to be a self-sufficient adult to the level they are able.

Needs and Wants of the Adult Children and the Family

In the economy of the last several years, there has been a growing segment of boomerang children. It has not been possible for the children to be self-supportive for many reasons. Moreover, we have also seen boomerang parents who are unemployed or retired and cannot be self-sufficient. Cooperation among the family members is crucial when these situations arise. The needs and wants of the individual family members must be considered in light of the total family unit. If these discussions have never occurred, conversations can turn into highly emotional events.

Emotions are constantly involved with needs and wants. Emotions are the human element. As humans, we have a brain, which allows us to make decisions. Variables enter into those decisions, and flexibility is necessary. Those variables include the relationships and emotional factors involved, whether it is a need or a want.

Everyone needs to know what their personal truths are. Children learn what is important to them as they grow, and they learn primarily from their own families. As they grow, they realize that they may disagree with the personal truths of their families. This is all part of the development of personal values. These values constantly evolve from birth. Good or bad, it's the foundation. It can be altered and increased, but the foundation remains, and it's as strong as any brick wall can be.

Our body of knowledge evolved from our families and other sources of support as we grew. It may sound like we have a great deal of information on how to make decisions about money. But let's add one more variable: human emotion. The emotion creates the energy—positive or negative—that flows through us every moment of our life.

Parents have a significant role and responsibility in building their children's confidence and self-esteem as it becomes incorporated into their body of knowledge. Decision making about money is a part of this, and parents can begin the process by working with their children to understand the difference between needs and wants in everyday family life. Each child is different; every parent teaches differently. It is the parent who knows each child best and can communicate effectively to reach the child. This interaction between parent and child has a lifelong impact.

The optimal time for this interaction to start is preschool. Once children enter school, they can be easily swayed as they begin to develop their body of knowledge. Yes, the parents should stay involved with the discussion, but basic economic concepts are beginning to be taught in elementary and secondary schools. The more discussion and education the child has, the higher the level of confidence and self-esteem the child will have, and the lower the anxiety level will be regarding money. Anxiety and the resulting stress about money are quite common! Knowing the distinction between a need and a want is the starting point for our personal body of knowledge. Being aware of the role emotions play with each need and want allows us to filter how we make decisions and the money involved in those decisions.

Another powerful influence on our body of knowledge is advertising: television, radio, and social media. Advertising permeates every moment of our life and affects our body of knowledge.

No matter the age, working with needs and wants is quite effective in developing decision-making skills about money. Developing these skills leads to financial wellness. Upon developing these skills, financial literacy with banking and investing is a natural progression.

Transformational Opportunity #1

This is your first opportunity to use a Money Journal. The more you invest in every activity as you move forward on this journey, the more you will begin to feel your emotions and their effect on your relationship with money. Get out your Money Journal and complete each item on this list.

1. Make a list of your physical needs, including everything that you could not live without.
2. Observe where your physical needs might actually be wants.
3. Make choices and finalize your list of needs.

These are the *needs* that you must cover with the money you have available to you.

Keep this list handy for reference as you move ahead.

Transformational Opportunity #2

Begin to use your Gratitude Journal. Jot down the things on your needs list that you created that you are grateful for. This is also a good time to listen to *Practices for Living from the Overflow, True Abundance,* a 2-CD set from "Sounds True", featuring Michael Bernard Beckwith. Check with your local bookstore or library for availability.

The list of needs you created in the first Transformational Opportunity is your first step on your path to becoming well-grounded in making decisions about money. Do these exercises consciously, and the skills that you will develop will form the foundation for making comfortable money decisions going forward.

Transformational Opportunity #3

1. Using your Money Journal, make a list of 100 wants.
2. If you do not have 100 wants, that is perfectly fine; you may or may not want to add items to the list later.

3. Next to each item on your list, write down how you "feel" when you say the item aloud. Feelings are important when you think and talk about money. They reflect your energy at that moment.

4. Pay close attention to the feeling you identified. This tells you how you really "feel" about having that item.

5. Now, prioritize your list from 1 to 100 with 1 being the most important to you.

6. Take your top 10 and create a new list.

7. With your top 10 list of wants, list the estimated price of each item as well as where you will find the money to pay for it. Be realistic.

8. Now, pick your #1 top want and move on to create "A Promise to Myself".

A Promise to Myself

My #1 Top Want

Is:_____

It's Very Important to Me Because:

_____

_____

_____

_____

_____

The Item Costs $_____and I will get it

From (Source) _____

By (Date) _____

This is my promise to myself.

(Signature) _____

Make as many copies as you need over time.

How does creating the promise to yourself feel? You have promised yourself that you will have your #1 want by a certain date.

You may find it helpful to begin gathering information for a personal spending plan in your Money Journal. Make sure that it includes everything on your list of needs as well as your #1 want. It is important to include the want because when you have wants, you have dreams, which allows yourself to have hope. You need to have hope as it is an energizing force of life!

So, know that you will fulfill all you need, want, and hope for!

Money Needs Energy

"We are unlimited beings. We have no ceiling. The capabilities, the talents, the gifts, and the power that is within everyone are unlimited."

Michael Beckwith

Your life is energy. You are a soul. You are a feeling. Money is also a feeling: wealth, security, flow, success, importance, special, power, peace. They are psychological aspects that you can feel. Money can make you feel self-sufficient; it can empower you!

What does it take to make you feel self-sufficient? What is your definition of sufficiency? Does "more" make you happier?

Transformational Opportunity #4

Define in your money journal what happiness means to you!

Observe yourself. Listen to how you talk about money. How do you make decisions about money? Who do you *want to be* with your money? Who do you *need to be* with your money?

In the September 2011 issue of *Whole Living* magazine, Debbie Lacy outlined job descriptions for your money in her article "Does

Your Money Need a New Job?" She then defines the various 'job descriptions' as follows:

The Security Guard: protects and maintains my well-being and that of my family.

The Personal Stylist: makes me look good, feel lovable, valuable, confident, and powerful.

The Genie: grants my wishes and funds my dreams.

The Day Laborer: shows up in the nick of time, pays the bills and the rent, supplies the food, and lets me make it from paycheck to paycheck.

Which of these job descriptions fit how you regard your money?

From the above job descriptions for your money, write in your Money Journal the present job description your money has; then write down a new job description if you were to give your money a promotion.

How is your money working for you? Are you a dollaraire or are you a millionaire?

The life you live now with the money you have will be the legacy you leave. Do you want it to be a legacy of sufficiency or a legacy of scarcity? Would you like to be living a life of "enough"?

Enough, Sufficiency, and More

"Enough" is tricky to define because, while it is dependent upon an individual's needs and wants, there is a point where a sense of fullness arrives – whether it be physical, mental or emotional. On the other hand, there are times when enough never seems 'enough'. Sometimes it becomes hoarding which can draw attention to the individual and the reasons for keeping everything. On the other hand, 'enough' is sometimes sought to live a life of chosen simplicity. "Sufficiency" is another term for "simplicity" and is a minimalist choice.

Your choices are personal. Fear of lack can drive the choice. In fact, the feelings of love or fear can be involved.

When you think of sufficiency, how do you feel? Sufficiency is a type of personal sustainability. You have enough to take care of your physical needs, and you have safety, love, and self-esteem.

Can you commit yourself to be happy with having enough? You may notice that you complain less if you do. You may also find that you have gratitude for what you have, and envy may disappear from your life.

Think about this: What do you *really need*?

Being in the Flow Will Transform You.

Transformational Opportunities will get you flowing through this Chapter... It is time for you to really begin to *feel*!

Transformational Opportunity #5

With your Money Journal, jot down your money thoughts, whatever they are, as you think about them. It is important to allow both positive and negative thoughts to emerge. The thoughts will flow to you as you do this, but to get started, here are some ideas:

1. What does your money mean to you?
2. What does love mean to you?
3. What does fear mean to you?
4. What is "enough" money for you?
5. What does sufficiency mean to you?

Patterns will begin to emerge as you continue to record your thoughts around money. Positive patterns will bring more positive thoughts, while negative patterns will bring more negative thoughts. Use your energy appropriately to address both positive and negative thoughts. Negative thoughts and patterns should be addressed rather than avoided. Begin to use your energy to address both the positive and negative!

When negative thoughts and patterns are addressed, they can be processed mentally and emotionally one by one. If they are left alone, they can become not only thoughts but also reality in your life. Clear your mind of negative thoughts and patterns. One at a time!

Transformational Opportunity #6

Your next step is with your Gratitude Journal. Write down three things you are grateful for every day. This can be a person, a place, or a thing.

Once you begin the daily gratitude entries, you may realize many things. The abundance of Planet Earth may become more apparent. The availability of everyday things will start to come into view. The Law of Abundance is God-given, and it is so very natural in everything. Abundance flows, and it has nothing to do with money.

Gratitude is one way of recognizing and telling your mind that you are rich in all things. Put away any thoughts of lack. It is time to learn that money is good. Greed is not good, but money is good.

Start to align your feelings with only good thoughts of money. When you stay close to your feelings, you will begin to stay in the flow, with money and everything in your life. Staying in the flow can be accomplished by staying in the present moment. Be aware of your feelings and be flexible–so you can shift and change.

How I Found "Flow"

Being in the flow is important to me. So it's ironic that I wrote these words a long time ago and I've had to do exactly what I've been talking about.

A fantastic position opened at Oberlin College in Ohio. The role was Special Assistant to the President for Community & Government Relations and was perfect for my background and what I love to do. Ironically, long before I learned about the postion, I decided to move to Oberlin within the year. So many things about the town appealed to me. It is walkable, supportive of local food and local entrepreneurial ventures, and strives to be environmentally friendly. It has an art museum, a music conservatory, and a fantastic theatre. I had wanted to live there for years, and I was moving towards making that a reality. While it was my intent to continue with my *Empower Excellence* work, it was a position that held great interest for me.

I have a strong belief that things happen the way they're supposed to, and I believed that if this position did not become mine, I would focus 100% of my energy on *Empower Excellence*. That would be the sign from the Universe and God that this was my work to do.

Here is the letter I received:

"Dear Jan,

Thank you for your interest in the position of Special Assistant to the President for Community and Government Relations at Oberlin College. Unfortunately, your application will not move to the next stage.

Sincerely,

Jane Mathison, Chief of Staff"

Devastated describes my feelings at that time!

I came back to my desk, wrote an email to those who were aware of my interest and those who had been my references, and then came right back to working on *Empower Excellence* as I knew this would be the outcome. I needed the final confirmation that was what I was supposed to focus on, and I had received it. My point is that I was able to stay in the flow, and be flexible, even if what I wanted didn't occur! Remember, be flexible and stay in the flow.

Being in the flow is a feeling of being alive, aware, and knowing that you can step fearlessly forward. You will discover a part of yourself that you're normally not aware of.

You can think of flow as love in action. It is a force of compassion. It is your divine light, your Spirit within, and your heart in action.

When you are in the flow, you will find yourself giving of your heart. You will find yourself returning to your soul where your divinity resides since the beginning of time. Flow is high energy that brings you a sense of security that grows more and more as you nurture yourself. Know that working on you is solid metaphysics and a powerful ethic.

From my experience today and throughout my life, being in the flow is a fantastic feeling. If you are not in the flow, you will sense immediately that it is missing. The flow plugs you into a deeper source of energy and passion. It is an impulse that allows you to create in a way that the Universe did billions of years ago. Amazing!

A lack of flow is low energy. It is fear!

Yes, you can feel the flow. Money flows when you are in the flow and when you are in a positive frame of mind. Your energy, and the energy of your money is where your feelings exist.

The Ego's Role in Money

The ego is another influence on your feelings around money. Although money makes the ego feel 'special', it also puts distance between you and others. If you detach from your ego, you no longer need others to admire you because of your money. When that happens, you can then relax with money. That is a true place of freedom. It is the place where you can go back easily to your Source, and you are no longer separate or distanced from everyone else. We are all one when we are connected to our Source.

Losing the Connection with Your Inner Child

While it's essential to deal with money and the decisions around money as an adult, you must not disconnect from your Inner Child. Your Inner Child is your creative force. The more creative you are, the more money is attracted to you. The creative side is the feminine side: soft and feeling. Embrace your childlike creativity and beauty. Think of embracing money as the creative and beautiful part of your life. Keep it simple; go back to your inner child!

When you are not in the flow, you may find yourself to be more serious. Seriousness is a disease of the ego and can warp your life, disconnecting you from your inner child. Going back to your inner child and learning how to keep it happy is an essential step in this transformative journey. Here are some ways to reclaim your inner child:

- Be fearless and take action.
- Gently toss out of your life what is not needed. Things that you do not need are a drain on you.
- Distance yourself from people who are not healthy. They are also a drain.
- Manage your time by getting rid of excessive commitments.
- Keep it simple.
- Do not compete because competition demonstrates lack. Once you raise your energy, competition will make no sense to you.

Emotional Flow

As you proceed in the flow, you will begin to give of yourself emotionally rather than constantly worrying about giving monetarily. People around you need your emotional support. But you cannot give them emotional support until you give yourself the emotional support you need. As you do this, you will also begin to accept and appreciate the emotional support of others.

By sharing my rejection from Oberlin College with so many people I had supported in the past, they in turn sent email notes supporting my work with *Empower Excellence*. I am fortunate to have supportive people in my life, and for that, I am grateful.

Never refuse to receive. By using your Gratitude Journal, you will draw abundance to yourself. Receive it graciously and with gratitude!

As your positive energy grows, you will find yourself feeling lighter. You will be more in the light of life. As you do this, you will find your truth, and you cannot hide from the truth. As you work out your feelings with money, and return to your authentic self, you will begin to take full responsibility for your decisions with money.

Your Light Within

This light is the Spirit you were when you entered the world as a newborn baby. Your memory of yourself at the time of your birth, as a Spirit, is a distant memory. Along the road, you experienced feelings of shame. As you pursue this journey of finding your true self, you will learn to leave shame behind you so you can find your

Spirit again. You will learn to leave the fear of dying, and the low energy that comes with it, behind you.

You will move into higher energy of love and living. As you do, you will return to your true spiritual energy and the energy of your life force. One of the symbols of your life force is money. This is energy and money is energy.

As you become more connected to your true self, you can focus more of your energy on what you *truly need* and who you authentically want to become. The ego gets set aside. You accept yourself, believe in yourself, and have high self-esteem.

Transformational Opportunity #7

As you begin to find your energy around money, it is helpful to turn to guidelines created by those who have gone before us. As a student of Unity (The Association of Unity Churches International), I have learned much from one of our founders, Charles Fillmore. There are areas that Charles Fillmore has cited over time that affect our feelings about money, such as love, fear, metaphysics, money, peace, power, and transforming energy. Meditate on each of his phrases. There is no need to know anything about Unity to do this exercise. Read each phrase aloud and then give the words some quiet thought.

1. Spiritual Substance is the Fundamental Basis of the Universe.
2. Spiritual Mind is the Omnipresent Directive Principal of Prosperity.

3. Faith in the Invisible Substance is the Key to Demonstration.
4. Man is the Inlet and Outlet of Divine Mind.
5. There is a Natural Law that Governs the Manifestation of Supply.
6. Wealth of Mind Expresses Itself in Riches.
7. God Has Provided Prosperity for Every Home.
8. God Will Pay Your Debts.
9. Tithing is the Road to Prosperity.
10. Right Giving is the Key to Abundance Receiving.
11. Laying up Treasure!
12. Overcoming the Thought of Lack: Letting Go of the Past and Overcoming the Thought of Lack is Germane to All that Follows.

Does Your Energy Want You to Be Rich?

"If you are to become rich in a scientific and certain way, you must rise entirely out of the competitive thought. You must never think for a moment that the supply is limited." Wallace Wattles

Way back in 1910, Wallace Wattles, in his book *The Science of Getting Rich*, gave us the following thought:

"It is perfectly right that you should desire to be rich; if you are a normal man or woman, you cannot help doing so. It is perfectly right that you should give your best attention to the Science of Getting Rich, for it is the noblest and most necessary of all studies. If you neglect this study, you are derelict in your duty to yourself, to God and humanity; for you can render to God and humanity no greater service than to make the most of yourself."

Money is everywhere. It crosses all boundaries, languages, and cultures. Money is neither good nor bad. It can be the instrument behind any conflict, disaster, or crisis.

Envision your possibilities.

- What would you like to do in your life?
- Who are the people you want to spend time with?

- Where are the places you want to go?
- Where would you like to call 'home'?
- What will allow you to be healthy and active?
- Do you want to make a difference?
- What will help you create your happiness?

While money alone does not buy you happiness, money is indeed an instrument to help you achieve it.

Life is a journey with unexpected twists and turns, and if we look at money as a companion on that journey, I think it should be a peaceful companion!

Before you go one step further on life's journey, look within. Are you living in the moment? At this moment, do you have the courage look within and bring forth that which has meaning within your heart? If so, you will find that this is a soulful moment.

Now add knowledge about money. Acquiring information and advice about money is easy. That includes what you learn from this book as well as other resources. Add it to your personal body of knowledge as you strive to reach a state of power with your money.

Time to Act

There is more. It is now time to act with wisdom and knowledge, and this can be tricky. But it's time to do something that improves your life, the life of your family, and those you love.

Take a moment and note what you may be feeling inside. It could be that you are beginning to feel the energy of money in your life.

There will be obstacles that pop up in your mind. Do not be stopped by these obstacles.

Money can be an uncomfortable subject. Some people will not even give any significant thought to money because it is too uncomfortable for them. You can choose to love money, or you can choose to hate money! Ignoring or avoiding negative feelings around money will not give you empowerment in your life. No matter how you feel, working with money is inevitable, for it truly does touch all parts of your life.

Work with money from the source of your true being. When you do, you begin to work with money in a way that gives you peace and power. That is when money allows you to feel connected with your heart, mind, and soul. So how can you start to take action right now?

If you take your work with money seriously, you will go within and find your authentic self and your Divine Mind, and you will emerge to resume your true-life journey with the peace and power within you. Your Divine Mind is a personal definition. It can be God, Buddha, Source, Inner Being. Anything that guides you internally can define your Divine Mind.

Transformational Opportunity #8

In your Money Journal, begin this work:

1. Start by defining your Life's Intentions.
2. Define your values- what is important in life?
3. Pay attention to the type of energy you have when it involves money.

4. Make conscious decisions to achieve the previous three items.

5. Keep reading and working with this book.

You have begun your money journey. It is no longer *one day*, or *someday*…it is *today*!

No matter if the emotions of fear, anger, or shame have kept you from your authentic action to move forward with your relationship with money, you will feel yourself moving now.

Be Ready for Conflict: The Red Boxing Gloves

"The possibility of rich relationships exists all around you — you simply have to open your eyes, open your mouth, and, most importantly, open your heart."

Cheryl Richardson

Visualize a pair of bright red boxing gloves on a table in front of you. Yes, I actually have a pair of bright red boxing gloves!

It's amazing how the Universe brings things like red boxing gloves into our lives. As a financial planner, I was given boxing gloves as the prize in a sales contest. When I left the business, I almost left them with the company but at the last moment brought them with me. I had no idea how, or if, I would ever have a reason to use them, but I have!

One of the gloves represents love, while the other represents fear. Love and fear are polar opposites and yet very connected. There are two basic emotions—love and fear. Anyone can act out of love or out of fear. It is that simple.

It also represents the barest emotions people feel about money in their life. If they act out of love or out of fear, it controls the energy surrounding their money.

In my workshops on energy and money, the red gloves are carefully positioned on the table with the thumbs facing outward, almost in opposing directions. As the workshop begins, I pass them around from person to person, allowing each to place the boxing gloves on their hands. A slight transformation can be seen in each person as they tune into their feelings about money, whether it is a feeling of love or fear.

The gloves are awkward for most as they struggle to put them on, stretching and pulling them into place. Once they put them on, I ask them to use the gloves to demonstrate their feelings about money at that moment. "Do they love or fear money?"

Remember that one glove represents love; one glove represents fear. At times, there is an awkward pause. Their answers range from the simplistic "love," "fear," or "love and fear." Many complicated stories explain their answers.

The boxing gloves are new to most who participate. It is an eye-opening moment for them, and it does demand focus on what money is in their lives. Is it love or is it fear, or a combination of both? It doesn't matter what the feelings are at that moment. It is a simple step to help them realize that money does have energy and they feel it when they answer the question in the workshop: "Do they love or fear money?'

Energy can be positive when it comes from a source of love, or negative coming from a source of fear. The question can then be asked: "What is the source of our energy?"

Simply put, the source of all is God. Source energy is always present. Energy is there. We know that energy can be good or bad or downright ugly! It is up to us to become aware of our inner source and our own personal energy. It is up to us to determine if our personal energy is good, bad, or ugly. When your energy doesn't feel quite right, you can learn to realign yourself with your *feel good* energy by asking "What is the source of this energy?" and focusing on the good in your life.

As a newborn, you experienced your first fear of life. The journey out of the womb, the birthing process, is a change of energy. While you were within your mother's uterus, you were safe, fed, and your birth mother nurtured you in every way. Then without much warning, you began your journey through the birth canal, dark and unknown to you, to the light of what you would come to know as life. Energy started the process, and it carried you through to your birth.

When you were born, you hopefully had all you needed to survive. Maybe you didn't. In either case, you quickly learned how to use your energy to make sure that you were fed, kept safe, and continue the journey of your lifetime. You found your energy and it was there for you to use. Most parents learn how to respond to their child's needs. As you grew, you learned the ways to use your energy for survival. Sometimes it was out of love, and sometimes it was out of fear.

In the *Dark Side of The Light Chasers*, Debbie Ford expands on this in a very brilliant way. Her writing illuminates how you grow positively out of love or negatively out of fear. It starts at birth and continues throughout your life. It is up to you to determine where your energy is at any given moment and then shift to the energy you desire. You can replace fear and frustration with hope and excitement and take it one step further to abundance and fulfillment. But, on the other hand, you can stay stuck in fear only to realize that by not moving, by not taking any risk, you risk all that life has to offer.

As you grow, you acquire feelings and emotions that affect your energy. As a result, you tend to behave in ways that will keep you safe. You adopt the energy of your parents, your family, your friends, your teachers, and your religious leaders.

Is all your energy positive? Of course not. It would be wonderful if it were. It would be awesome if we all felt we are all truly unique. It would be amazing if you had all the tools that would allow you to make sure that you kept all the power and self-esteem you had when you were born.

Dr. Wayne Dyer and Kristina Tracy co-authored *Incredible You*, and they simplified self-esteem into ten ways to let your greatness shine through as a child:

1. Share the good.
2. Find what you love.
3. You are filled with love.
4. Find a quiet place inside.
5. Make today great!
6. Change your thoughts to good.
7. Take care of yourself.
8. Picture what you want.

9. Everyone is special, especially you!

10. Good thoughts give you energy.

While this is not new, you need to be reminded of these basic thoughts. We know this, and we know that most people are well-intentioned. Yet, it does not matter. Our self-esteem is compromised. Love, the foundation of all goodness, is something we are born with and is sometimes replaced by fear. Fear can be in so many parts of your life. Sometimes you know that fear is there, and sometimes you don't. And not everyone is well-intentioned!

Before you realize it, your childhood is gone. You become an adult, life is busy, and you may have children, or even grandchildren, of your own. You have become a composite of all that has been in your life. It can be good or bad, love or fear, right or wrong! You may feel that your life is not what you wanted it to be. So how do you get back to a point in your life where you had hope for your future life? Do you know what your life could be?

Think about the red boxing gloves. Visualize putting them on. Take the time to feel them while you are putting them on then ask yourself, "What does money mean to me at this moment?"

Step by step, release all emotions, surrender to your inner strength, and energize yourself to answer that question at this moment. That is the only energy you need right now. Whether it is based on love or fear, accept the feelings and energy for what it is and begin the journey to create the energy you dream of for your life.

Should you be tempted to give it up, keep the image of the red boxing gloves in your mind's eye. The red boxing gloves, representing love and fear, can lead you to a place of peace throughout your journey and show you just how incredible you really are. They can show you how money can be the energy you need in all aspects of your life.

Typically, boxing gloves are usually thought of in the context of a boxing match. Of course, you can win this match. But first, you must take the time to put on the red boxing gloves. Then you must draw on all your energy to have love be victorious over fear in your feelings about money and replace those feelings with peace and power.

Emotions with money are not easy. So, when your time with the red boxing gloves ends, think back to the beginning of the chapter where the boxing gloves are on the table with the thumbs facing outward in opposing directions.

When the gloves are put back at the end of my workshop, their thumbs rest facing each other, interlocked for their next match with love and fear. It's amazing how the energy shifts in just a few hours as each participant has truly looked within to connect with their money energy.

Money: A Symbol of Life Force Energy

"If you believe it, if you can see it, if you act from it, it will show up for you. That's the truth."

Michael Beckwith

Think of money as a magnet attracting good to those who have it.

Can you stay healthy without money to buy good food or the seeds to plant it? Can you keep yourself and your family sheltered without money to pay your rent or to pay your mortgage? Can you provide a necessity, like water, without the funds to pay for your home's water bill?

These are just a few of the basic needs that require money.

Money developed over time as a form of exchange to cover basic needs. It wasn't meant to be coveted or to be worshiped. It was meant to be a currency to measure what people owed each other for basic necessities.

Transformational Opportunity #9

Take a dollar bill from your wallet or purse, hold it, and feel its energy. Do you know where the dollar bill was before it came into your hands? Create a story for that dollar bill. Get in touch with your story, your feelings, and your emotions. Be creative. Know that this dollar bill has its own energy. Once it came into your possession, its energy came from you.

Now, in your Money Journal, write the story you have created for this dollar bill, including how it came into your possession and what it has done since it has been with you. Where is it intended to go?

Money of its own accord has no energy. Its energy comes from your Divine Source.

While money in its physical form is simply metal or paper, it has meaning and a relationship with your mind, heart, and soul. It can bring forth emotions, both love and fear, which is the metaphysical aspect of money. Once again, a simple definition of metaphysics is exploring beliefs and concepts above and beyond the simple physical realm.

The broader concept of prosperity and abundance includes the metaphysical aspect of money, especially the keys to prosperity and the stumbling blocks many people encounter.

Is the truth about money your truth about money? It may not necessarily be so. There may be adverse states of consciousness reeling within you right now. These states of consciousness can only be as powerful as the power and energy you allow. The secret lies in letting go of whatever the adverse state may be. You can withdraw the power you have given it, and once you do, the power will disappear.

How can you be sure that the power will disappear? You were born to succeed. It is the Divine intention that all people should be happy, healthy, and prosperous.

What is the truth about money? Money is energy, and there is an inexhaustible supply of prosperity or abundance available to you.

Accept that truth in thought, word, and action. That truth is a consciousness that perceives and knows there is an inexhaustible supply of prosperity or abundance. It is a realization backed by thoughts, words, and actions, and it is true regardless of outward appearances. It is a prosperity demonstration.

Eliminate the Fear

Whether it is a thought, an object, or a person hindering you in your quest for the truth about money in your life, there is fear underlying it. If you are timid or bury your talent, you are operating in fear.

Both prosperity and lack begin with a thought. If you are in a state of fear, clinging to old beliefs and old thoughts, you are unaware of your power. If you blame others or believe that a person has the power to hinder your prosperity, you are missing your power. If you are having miserly thoughts, hoarding, and fearing that you'll lose all that you have, be careful. The loss you dread will happen because that is the object of your focus!

Overcome this by moving from a state of fear to a state of love. Stop looking outside yourself and start looking within. Then you will be well on your way to finding the truth and the good in money, which is the ultimate reality of being happy, healthy, and successful. Good is love, truth and within all of us. There is never an end to the good; there is never an end to the truth. That is why the adverse power will disappear once you withdraw the power you have given it.

Let Go to Attract More

While it sounds counter to the concept of being in the flow of money, letting go of the attachment to money and material things opens the way to attract more prosperity and abundance.

Staying in a state of fear or lack pulls the focus from your inner Spirit. Focusing on your fear or lack increases its power. Instead, aim for nonresistance. When you're open to receiving, abundance and prosperity can flow. Practice nonresistance, and you will find good that will run to meet you. You will see goodness responding. You will persevere and prosper.

Move Out of Fear

When you focus on prosperity or blessings and stay centered on positive expectations, you are in a prosperity state of consciousness. It is then that an abundance of prosperity will appear! Thus, there is a direct relationship between prosperity, the joy of giving, and the joy of receiving.

What will move you out of fear? Quite simply, one suggestion is laughing! Laugh your fear away. Sing. Do affirmations. When your thoughts are anxious, fearful, or angry, you are in a lack of consciousness. So being joyful—laughing, singing, affirming—opens the way for you to experience prosperity.

You must create room for the prosperity that is yours. As Tony Robbins said, "The only impossible journey is the one you never begin." A lack of prosperity, caused by unforgiveness, is not a good place to find yourself. Forgive fully, fill your mind with thoughts of forgiveness and welcome empowering thoughts of love, justice, and peace.

As you grow in your prosperity consciousness and awareness of your Source, Spirit, and God, your need for things will decrease. You'll know that your needs will be met every day. Divine Order becomes a part of your finances. A rich consciousness will begin to reveal prosperity to you.

Through your powers of faith, wisdom, and understanding, you will begin to balance your needs and wants. Wastefulness will disappear. Draw upon your spiritual resources, your capabilities, your power to accomplish things. Look into your soul, as well as your conscious and unconscious mind, to appreciate all that you are. You will begin to express positivity in love which is the foundation for your inner peace. You will once again have the soulful peace you were born with.

Your soul will set your Divine Ideas, your spiritual focus, and prosperity into motion. Prosperity is an attitude and feeling. It is only a secondary attitude and feeling that concerns itself with money.

Your True Wealth

Your Divine Ideas are your only true wealth, and they are the primary source for all good in life. God is your Divine Mind. Your Divine Ideas are your prosperity and are always available through your faith, prayer, and meditation. As you join with Source through faith, prayer, and meditation, your mind becomes established in faith, harmony, and peace, and you are open to receive.

This receptivity is the result of Divine Mind working with time, attention, and intention to put Divine Ideas into action. Concentrating on abundance and prosperity, your Divine Ideas begin to work on good results. The realization of these results is very personal. Make the results yours. *It will change your finances. It will destroy your fears. It will stop your worries.*

All at once, there will be rejoicing in the bounty that God has made known to you which is your Law of Increase. It will eliminate anxious thoughts, and you will realize that your resources are unlimited. Then, feeling the perfect abandon of your original childlike nature, you will be in the flow! This is your truth at your core level of being!

Transformational Opportunity #10

Now it's time to express extreme gratitude in your Gratitude Journal. Invest your time in blessing and praise. Feel grateful! As you express gratitude and appreciation, you will experience many benefits. You will attract great relationships. You will release energy that will attract opportunities to you. You will be in the flow!

Praise what you have so that it increases the flow. This is Universal Substance! Now is the time for the power of your imagination to step forth to visualize, conceptualize, and see only the good. This is your abundance substance. Do it with patience and trust. All of this will ease the waiting period for your prosperity. Above all, be at peace with the process—and have faith!

Money Energy: Shifting Your Energy Through Faith

"You can never solve a problem with the same kind of thinking that created the problem in the first place."

Albert Einstein

Now that you are entering a realm of higher spiritual energy, please believe that everything you need will be provided. Your inner spark has been there all the time, but it was hidden. Your inner spiritual core of love, peace, rejoicing, cheerfulness, celebration, and kindness has always been there. Now, it's time to reawaken these Divine Ideas.

You are simply shifting from what is to that which you want. You are focusing on what you intend to bring about. It is not a quick fix, so don't complain, don't whine! Be patient with yourself. Demonstrate love throughout the process—love is the highest vibration that will keep you strong.

In 2010, Wayne Dyer wrote *The Shift*. He had three shifts in the book which relates to what is happening at this point of shifting your energy:

1. The Shift from Entitlement to Humility
2. The Shift from Control to Trust
3. The Shift from Attachment to Letting Go

The shifts are important, and you need to take the time to incorporate them into your life. Only humans use this creative process. It awakens us to our spiritual impulse and to our intuition.

It is the impulse, the seed we all share from The Big Bang! You are evolving. Do not be overwhelmed by the possibilities. Instead, be positive toward it and allow it to align you with the goodness of life. Be a part of the evolving conscience.

Andrew Cohen talks about this at great length in his thought-provoking work, *Evolutionary Enlightenment*. If you want to explore this, his work is a great place to start.

It is a miraculous process knowing who you are. It is God demonstrating through you as He continues creating the Universe. The evolution is God's intention and is occurring through you. It is awesome! Even though the world was created in The Big Bang, it has taken over 14 billion years to get to where we are today. I say we have a lot further to go individually and as the Universe!

Each of us has the power to be the 'one' individually, but we all have to be the 'One' collectively for God, as the Universe evolves through us. This spiritual development compels us to evolve and shifts us from ego to our authentic self, individually and collectively. Eventually, the ego is displaced. What remains is love. You can feel the emotion. Fear will begin to diminish, and healing begins. Can you feel it? Allow yourself to feel even the smallest feeling. Accept it. It is a simple process and a process that brings hope back into your life.

Yes, you will feel the emotion. It is like the seas, with its tides ebbing and flowing. You will feel the wind in your soul. I like to journal outside on my deck. It is a very private place where I can feel even the slightest breeze, which I truly believe is God speaking to me when I have hit on a powerful feeling in my journaling. It is a wonderful feeling being able to stop and feel even the breath of God through the wind. Find your wind!

You may be affected by a word, a smell, a song, a touch. While you are feeling all of this, know that these are feelings and emotions. Stay aware, balanced, and centered. Appreciate the emotions for what they are, even if they include fear. Know that the emotions are your guide to alert you that you may be drifting away from your path of love. If fear appears, mentally transform it, and regain hope!

This process of spiritual development is your personal evolution. Through this discovery of evolution, you are learning who you are. You are demonstrating your power of choice. Intentions become clearer. Your soul becomes active in commanding the energy that flows toward your ideals, commitments, and what you stand for. Your money has energy because of what the soul is sending its way. In a way, your money now has a soul.

Learn to draw on your own ever-present Source and its energy. By going to your inner being, you recognize the energy that underlies all your feelings. Align with your abundant Source and learn how to feel prosperous and deserving. Consciously, carry cash in your pocket. This simple act will make you feel abundant, prosperous, safe, secure, and positive.

Feeling positive will motivate you to act. That motivation will carry you through the following chapters on how to energize your money. Feel free to come back and visit these beginning chapters to bring you back to your center. You have now learned how to release and let go of the past and trust your Divine Mind. Whenever fear appears, and it will, return to love through these first pages.

Breathing in Love and Faith

"If you don't control what you think, you can't control what you do. Simply, self-discipline enables you to think first and act afterward."

Napoleon Hill

Welcome to your 'work'. You have been preparing for this, and now it is here. So let's begin the habit of breathing. Breathing is an automatic function that you depend on as a matter of life. When was the last time you really took the time to breathe? Take a moment to breathe, inhaling deeply through your nose. Follow the breath as it moves into your body. Now slowly exhale, again following the breath as it leaves your body. Breathe deeply. Do this at least three times.

Breathing is an important preliminary step to so many activities. Breathing makes you stop, pause, and take inventory before you clear your mind.

Let's get started on the work…

Transformational Opportunity #11

What is your biggest money issue? Write as much as you need to in your Money Journal.

When you feel completely satisfied with what you wrote, continue and ask yourself the following related questions. The answers should relate only to your *biggest money issue*.

1. Is it true that this is your biggest money issue?
2. Can you be certain—100% certain—that this is true?
3. Shift to the reverse of your biggest money issue. Pay attention to this.
4. Is the reverse true for you?
5. What payoffs are you getting from your biggest money issue?
6. What would your life look like without your biggest money issue?
7. Picture your life without your biggest money issue. Do not allow any excuses. How does that feel?
8. Notice your breathing. Are you breathing easier?
9. Bring all of this to your physical reality.
10. This can be difficult, and you may face resistance.
11. You are shifting your energy, and concern will happen.
12. Relax and breathe—this is an energy shift.
13. How will you continually reinforce how you feel following the energy shift?

Energizing yourself will continually reinforce the new you. In our earlier discussion on flow, how did you feel?

Transformational Opportunity #12

In your Money Journal, define 'flow' for yourself. Have you ever been in the flow? How did you feel? Flow is energy, and there are six forms of energy:

1. Money
2. Time
3. Physical Vitality
4. Enjoyment
5. Creativity
6. Support of Friends

Be at ease as you proceed through this exercise. However, if you do become uneasy, take the time to do the breathing exercise at the beginning of this chapter. When you are uneasy, you may experience a lot of chatter in your mind. Many people refer to this as "monkey mind". The goal is to find peace and power through this work. Whenever I refer to the chatter in your mind, a butterfly with its fluttering wings will be used as a metaphor. The butterfly is more calming.

Take a moment to think about this butterfly. Breathe and thank the butterfly for fluttering her wings in your mind. Let her know that you appreciate her beautiful sharing, then consciously move on.

Take as much time as you need to quiet your mind. Once it is quiet, we are going to look deeply at the circle of energy, on the back cover of this book, starting at the top. This is the starting point and where you are focusing your energy.

Focus on your biggest money issue from your Money Journal. Mentally and emotionally, put your energy here. Focusing on your most significant money issue is your first effort toward making a change. This step is the beginning of taking action.

Dwell in the moment and your feelings, which is the beginning of the stage of *Excellence* for you. Feel good about the action you have taken. Excellence leads to empowerment which is the next step in your energy shift. You were born empowered. Empower yourself again with the inner examination you have done and the excellence you have achieved.

When you empower yourself, you will create more energy, *magnified energy*, which is the last part of the energy circle. This *magnified energy* will take you to the next step toward resolving your biggest money issue.

Continue with small steps until you sense the feelings of peace return regarding this particular issue. Then, you should feel a shift in the energy. Your steps to peace can be prayer, journaling, reflection, or a discussion with a trusted person in your life and can be used with any issue in your life, whether it is money or something else.

Finish each cycle with three of the breathing exercises. Remember to breathe in deeply and to exhale completely. The energy circle is a good exercise to focus on as individual fears appear. Returning to the list of questions displayed in the discussion of the biggest money issue is also helpful.

Energize Your Money

Now that you have started focusing on your money issues, let's talk about energizing your money. There are some major areas that can affect your energy of money. They can affect them positively out of love or negatively out of fear. Think about these:

Your Job   Does it give you Financial Security?

Your Relationships   Does it give you Emotional Security?

A Trip to the Mall   Does it give you any Security?

Think about each of them. How do you feel about them? Are you uncomfortable? Does chatter start in your brain? Think about the butterfly. Her fluttering wings may represent fear to you or chatter in your mind, but ultimately, she represents peace and power with your money.

As you continue this inner work, you will find that you are greater than the chatter in your mind, no matter how loud it becomes. Your goal is to stop the chatter in your mind when you think about money. Here are some easy steps to accomplish this goal:

1. Look. Where are you with money? Make this your focus.
2. See the truth. Where do you want to go with money?
3. Act! Clean up your past and move forward.

You need to be honest with yourself as you do these exercises. However, you also need to be truthful. There is a difference between honesty, which includes feelings, justifications, judgements, and thoughts vs. truth, which are simply the facts.

Transformational Opportunity #13

It is time to write the story of *Your Life with Money*!

In your Money Journal, begin writing, starting with your very first memory surrounding money. Be honest and be sure to include the truth. Both the feelings and the facts are important. Then look back on your life and see what you can recall. Some important memories may comet to the surface, and you will find yourself revisiting sections many times over, which is an important activity.

When these memories are brought to the surface, they can be released. The process of letting go is necessary before you can establish a relationship with money that will be peaceful and powerful. Let's start writing. Don't forget to breathe!

Letting Go!

"The truth simply is, and it survives, believe it or not. Lies need me to believe them. If I don't believe lies, they don't survive my skepticism, and they simply disappear."

Don Miguel Ruiz

Now that you are examining your relationship with money, you will find that you will revise your money story periodically as new memories return to you. Your intentions and integrity will flow easier as your feelings and values cone to the surface.

Transformational Opportunity #14

Think about the following questions:

1. Who do you *pretend* you are?
2. Who are you *afraid* you are?
3. Who are you *really*?

The third question, "Who are you really?" addresses your authentic self. Take the time to answer all three of the questions in your Money Journal. Consider your values when you answer these questions. *Who are you really?*

There are no right or wrong answers to the questions. Simply list the words that you believe describe you. The following are just examples:

Honest

Compassionate

Caring

Reliable

Loving

Dependable

Spiritual

Healthy

Generous

Charitable

Hopeful

Faithful

Inspired

Inspiring

Deep

True

Truthful

Soulful

Rich

Attractive

Purposeful

Dynamic

Happy

This list is not all inclusive. These are your words, your values, and standards.

Now, read each word aloud. Notice the emotions that come up when you read them aloud—love or fear? Write down the feeling next to the word in your Money Journal. Don't rush the process. Where you find fear, make a special note to return to the word and work on the feeling until you replace the fear with love. Spend as much time as necessary with the list of your values and standards—you choose what to call them—so that you feel confident that these words totally and truthfully describe who you are within your Spirit. These values are your guides as to where you need to work with the energy of your money. Then, when you feel good with the results, move forward. You are now in the process of freeing up your energy from any negative thoughts about yourself you may discover now and in the future.

Take the time to breathe as you do this work. Breathing gives you a positive source of energy as you work through the activities. When you do move forward, know that you have everything you need to work on to shift your energy with money. You have had all you need since your birth. As a newborn baby, that was the real you. It's time to recapture the real you to realize your dreams.

What are your dreams? What are your goals? What are your intentions? Know that you are capable of achieving them as your destiny.

Transformational Opportunity #15

The time is now! Take the time you need to think about this. Write in your Money Journal what you have dreamt of during your life. Which ones have you achieved? Which ones are still out there?

Make a list in your Money Journal of all the dreams that remain in your life. List every single one. Don't omit anything. This is not an exercise to justify anything. Rather, it's an exercise to acknowledge your dreams.

Allow Yourself to Dream!

Review your list of dreams and choose the biggest, most important one that will make you feel so much love. In your Money Journal, go back to your childhood, and find your crayons for this activity. Draw a picture that represents the biggest, most important dream of your childhood. Do not make excuses. Instead, allow yourself this dream! Take time to do this, and embrace the feelings that come up, write them down, and share it with someone you trust. Put it into words and enjoy the moment!

Make Your Dreams Come True

"We all possess more power and greater responsibilities than we realize, and visualizing is one of the greatest of these powers." Genevieve Behrend

Why do some people cringe when asked about their goals? Why do they flinch when they're asked to write them down? It's essential to write your dreams down on paper so you can set goals and make them real.

Whims and Anchors

Whims are the trivial, frivolous things in life that make us smile. Just say the word "Whim". It makes you smile because it represents fun, fairy dust, and something whimsical. As you continue your work with your money relationship, Whims represent your wants.

Anchors represent stability, keeping you in place like a boat at sea. Anchors are necessary and not anywhere near as much fun as Whims. Anchors are closely tied to our serious intentions in life and can be a strong conduit for energy. Most importantly Anchors represent our needs.

Both whims and anchors can be goals and those goals should be SMART.

Specific

Measurable

Attainable

Relevant, Realistic, Real

Time-Based

When you work on your goals, they should be positive and based on love, not fear.

Transformational Opportunity #16

Goals, goals, goals… Everyone Needs Goals!

1. List each goal you have for your life.
2. Make each goal SMART.

Don't stress over your goals. You can work on them again when the energy is right. Your goals are not a 'to-do' list. As you write your goals, let them come from your heart and nurture your Spirit. Your goals should come from deep in your soul. They should excite you and be fun to create. It doesn't matter if they are whims or anchors. Either way, they should represent what you really want in life.

Busy, Busy, Busy... Stop it!

> *"Don't judge each day by the harvest you reap, but by the seeds that you plant."*
>
> Robert Louis Stevenson

Are you always busy? When you were growing up, did your parents and teachers insist that you always be doing *something*? We try too hard to live. It is amazing that, as adults, we "work" to relax, sleep, have downtime, go on vacation, or even daydream. Yet, all of those activities have been proven to contribute to health and wellbeing.

Is your mind constantly chattering away about what you should or could be doing? No wonder you are confused. The chatter in your mind is closely related to what I call *driven behavior*. A behavior that doesn't just suddenly appear when you are an adult. It's learned over your lifetime, and it takes a while to overcome. So breathe, and think of the butterfly!

When you *Set This Butterfly Free*, you are learning how to *simply be*. You have a process now to change your energy with money and with life! You have carefully worked on your intentions, your dreams, and your goals. However, is the road to achieving them smooth and full of light? Maybe, maybe not. There may be outer and inner blocks to progress.

Inner Blocks to Progress

We may blame external events or situations as blocks to our progress. The more complicated the blocks are, the more we have internalized them as part of our driven behavior. Examining those internal blocks is a critical step. Remember, observing your behavior involves:

1. Look
2. See the truth
3. Take Action
4. I'm adding a fourth step:
5. Face Your Fear!

It's essential to be 100% authentic, which means you can give permit yourself to feel joy. Joy can be the catalyst to ending the driven behavior.

Driven behavior includes:

- Guilt
- Exhaustion
- Resentment
- Loss of Interest
- Perfectionism
- Addictive or Compulsive behavior

- Overspending
- Binging
- Purging
- Gambling
- Workaholic tendencies

Transformational Opportunity #17

In your Money Journal, write your definition of each of the words in the previous list. Then slowly read each word aloud, taking the time to feel the sound of the word. What does it stir up in your Spirit? Note in your Money Journal any word that stirs up strong feelings and identify whether they are feelings of love or fear.

Did you react strongly to any of the words? If so, spend some time reflecting on why you felt the way you did as it will take you back to your authentic self. This process is about finding peace and power instead of being 'busy' all the time. Being busy is driven by fear, not by love. Love is what leads to peace. You can be busy at times but just be aware if it's the result of driven behavior that stems from fear.

Butterflies Are Meant to Be Free

"Every word in my mind is just a symbol, and symbols aren't real. They're my creation; they're my art. I am the one who gives meaning and power to every word. Words are just a tool for me to communicate."

Don Miguel Ruiz

We replaced the chattering monkey mind with the butterfly's fluttering wings as a more peaceful symbol several chapters back. Even the butterfly's fluttering wings can be a distraction, and you may worry if you are doing the right thing when it comes to money. As long as there is fluttering, you are not confident about your relationship with money.

You have done a lot of work to learn your true feelings, which can quiet the fluttering wings. Now, you need to make a choice. You can either fly around with the fluttering wings of the butterfly or begin to fly with your dreams. Where is your energy with money? Is it in your mind? Is it in your Spirit? Outward energy is action. Inward energy is the fluttering butterfly wings.

What will your flight look like: flying with a frenzied butterfly or the peaceful flight as your dreams take off? Butterflies are meant to be free. If those butterfly wings are still fluttering and flapping, you are not confident in making your money decisions. You may still be making excuses. You may still be a little paranoid. You may still be rationalizing. You may still be defensive. Maybe you are still a victim or a martyr. So start taking back your energy, your life, and your power.

Transformational Opportunity #18

It is time to confront the fluttering and flapping butterfly wings. After a few days of journaling all your money thoughts, you may be ready to tell the butterfly that it is time to fly away. Trust me, give it time and you will be prepared to say "goodbye" in no time!

In your Money Journal, write down every thought about money that you have. No matter if it is good, bad, silly, angry, impulsive, or paranoid. It is slightly exhausting when you *look, see the truth, and act*. Are you feeling exhausted or drained? You could be. You are freeing the butterfly. The butterfly is simply a symbol of your transformation. This exercise will free the butterfly from your mind, although it is still concerned with you. The butterfly's job is not done until you are totally free in your energy with your money.

During this phase, you may feel alone for a while. However, your mind is becoming calm. You are going back to your first days of life when your thoughts were more straightforward. Rest with those thoughts. You are once again learning how your world works.

Congratulate yourself! You are turning down the noise in your mind. As a result, peace and power are being created. As you've gone through this book, you have discovered how your mind works with money. You're activating your 'money mind' in a healthy way. Your 'money mind' can now support your dreams and your goals with a new flight pattern that puts you on a path to peace and power with your money.

Determining Your Why

You may be the first in your family to change how you think about money. But do you really want to be different? Doesn't everyone have problems with money? Are you uncertain, unsettled, nervous, angry, happy? You have released old beliefs. You have the right to feel a little different.

The clean slate you now have, is the perfect place to begin your life with your 'money mind'. You can connect to your true feelings as you embrace your goals and dreams and develop your confidence and self-esteem. You are confidently making decisions that are in your best interest. You are doing this all by yourself now.

Transformational Opportunity #19

Continue to keep your Money Journal and write down all of your thoughts about money. You are in transition, and you will have conflicting thoughts. Allow those thoughts to come through, then release them as they come to the surface so you can move forward.

Emptying Our Mind

"...when we empty our mind of our ego-driven thoughts, we invite forgiveness into our hearts, and by letting go of the lower energies of hatred, shame, and revenge, we create a mind-set of problem resolution."

Wayne W. Dyer

Look in the mirror. See that person looking back at you? Is there anything you need to forgive that person for? Anything at all? Go back as far as you can remember. What do you need to forgive? Forgiveness starts with forgiving yourself! When you forgive, you become lighter emotionally.

Is there something that can trigger your emotions quickly? Talk about it. Start the process of forgiving by dismantling any negativity you harbor. This may take time, but you must dismantle it all. We talk about forgiveness, but what does forgiveness really mean? How do you begin to forgive? There is a fundamental way to approach forgiveness every day of your life. No matter how well you know someone, every time you meet them:

1. Think about what you say about the other person before you say it.

2. Be careful how you characterize (stereotype) them. First impressions do count.

3. Pretend that it is the first time.

4. Be gentle with your thoughts, your facial expressions, and, most importantly, your words.

5. Soften your words and soften your heart so you can halt negative thoughts.

6. Do not gossip

7. Be your authentic self!

8. Be courageous, be gentle, and be forgiving!

The result of all the work you have done so far is connecting you with yourself. You will be more in touch with your heart and your feelings. You know deep in your heart if there is anyone you need to forgive, including yourself. Know that, even if you forgive everyone right now, there may be more forgiveness necessary in the future. Live in a forgiving mode.

Fluttering and flapping butterfly wings may appear through this process as forgiveness brings up all kinds of thoughts from the past. That is fine, just thank the butterfly, and let it fly away!

Do not make a big production of forgiving. Instead, do it quietly and move on. There is no need to confront the person you are forgiving. That would make both of you uncomfortable. So do it by yourself and be gentle and kind.

With forgiveness, you are releasing issues from your past and freeing up energy that has been held back with old wounds. The result is good, positive energy. By not forgiving, you make excuses not to accomplish your dreams. The positive energy you are now creating will work to help you achieve your dreams. Celebrate!

Energy and Moving Forward

"A pessimist sees the difficulty in every opportunity; an optimist sees the opportunity in every difficulty."

Winston Churchill

Psychologists refer to our collection of facts and experiences as a structure of knowledge which has been developing since you were born. This structure of knowing helps define and clarify your world in conscious and unconscious ways. It is now time to expand your structure of knowledge.

If you are using your current structure of knowledge as an excuse in any way, you need to expand. If reluctance and fear block any desire to move forward on your path, you need to expand to experience joy and satisfaction daily. More than ever, if your future looks like your past, you need to expand. Once again, you need to *look, see the truth, and act.*

Transformational Opportunity #20

What is your structure of knowledge right now? Record your feelings in your Money Journal as you move forward:

1. Is your structure of knowledge keeping you from progressing?
2. What good points are there that you want to keep?
3. What bad points do you want to release?
4. Analyze all of this in the way you have learned from this work.
5. In your Money Journal, write down all the facts you know about money. How do you feel about all the points that you have listed?

Be flexible, be courageous. Be gentle. Question everything you know about money. Then observe your feelings. The flutter in your mind is gone but, the butterfly could return. Be aware.

Obstacles Are Not Negative

"Whenever you change your structure of knowledge, and your feelings about money, you are sure to have obstacles that will appear in your new life. They will be different for every person; they are very personal." Jan Litterst

Life constantly presents obstacles. When you encounter an obstacle, observe how you handle it. The more obstacles you encounter, the better you get at overcoming them. Obstacles are not harmful. In the metaphysical sense, obstacles acknowledge your intentions. If there is a breakdown of any sort when you encounter them, remember that they are simply acknowledgements of your new intentions.

You may think it's better if you do not encounter any obstacles. Think again. You may not be challenging yourself. Growth comes from facing and overcoming obstacles and challenges. Seek balance.

On the other hand, if you only encounter obstacles, you may be making things too hard for yourself, and it might be wise to pause and consider your intentions. Choosing your goals and intentions over your plans will add to your success. Of course, real-life plans can be modified, but your dreams usually aren't. So give that a moment of thought.

Next Steps

Thinking is just one step in facing your money mindset. You must act. It is time to check your credit score and to determine your net worth so you can accept your current state of affairs. You can get your credit score by going to sites like Equifax.com or CreditKarma.com. You can determine your net worth by going to a site such as Investopedia.com, Nerdwallet.com or Kiplinger.com. Once you get both numbers, document them, and notice how you feel about them. Then document the changes you are going to make to improve both of them. Track your feelings as you work to improve your credit score and build up your net worth. As you move through these tasks, learn to trust yourself, your intuition, and your judgment.

Energy and Gratitude

"Many people who order their lives rightly in all other ways are kept in poverty by their lack of gratitude."

Wallace Wattles

Quite simply, be grateful!

So many articles, books, songs, and more have been written about gratitude! It is quite possible that you may have your own definition of gratitude. When I think of gratitude, I hear "thank you" in my mind.

There are simple ways to shift the way you observe events in your life so that you can pump them full of gratitude. First, think about what you are grateful for, what you are thankful for; and then realize how much abundance you have in your life, whether it is money, material goods, or anything or anyone else.

Continue to fill your Gratitude Journal. You are well on your way to shedding your negative money feelings of the past and your positive money feelings moving forward. Much like exercising a muscle to make it stronger, you are using your energy to become positive when it comes to money. You are learning to trust yourself and how you feel.

You are working on some basic money tasks with your credit score and your net worth. You are on your way.

You have learned there are only two major emotions—love and fear—surrounding money. So maybe now, the red boxing gloves make sense. Love or fear. Which do you choose? You are now more confident about money and growing more every day. The longer you work with the concepts in this book, the more love you will feel about your money. Money no longer controls you. It is now a way to accomplish your dreams.

Your feelings about money, and your feelings about your thoughts about money, are changing. Go with the change! Your feelings will become more grounded in love. Even when you are fearful, it will not last as long as it did in the past. You have more feelings of pure love in your life, your mind, and your soul.

Your thoughts are the source of your feelings. It is that simple. Your energy forms from your feelings: Thoughts > Feelings > Energy

If you base your thoughts on love, you'll feel love, and your energy will be full of love as well.

Here's to a loving relationship with your money, a relationship that brings peace and power to you and your money!

Thank you for allowing me to be a part of your journey!

Breathe…Reflect…Transform…and Love!

About the Author

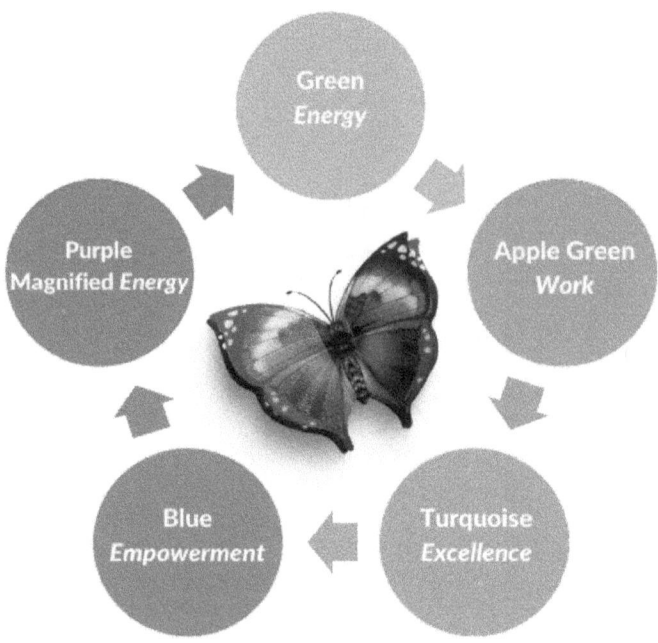

Jan Litterst, called the 'go-to' financial wellness expert in her community, with 20 years of experience in the financial services industry. She is a Financial Empowerment Strategist and the Founder of Empower Excellence where she helps individuals, groups and organizations improve their relationship with money.

www.ingramcontent.com/pod-product-compliance
Lightning Source LLC
Chambersburg PA
CBHW071113030426
42336CB00013BA/2067